W9-BSG-645

1997

Well mom—
Here is your book... or at least it will be when you start _and_ finish it. For years you have been lamenting the fact that you never wrote a book— now is the perfect time. You have three daughters, two grandchildren, and more to come. Start writing down memories so that all of us can share them with you.

write about your grandparents so that we may know them too... write about the first time you met dad... write about the first time you held each of your daughters... write about the first time you held your grandchildren... write about your summers working at the club. Basically, write about you... your thoughts, your feelings, your experiences. Well— I got you a _purple_ journal to motivate you... and one with quotations to motivate... now the rest is up to you. So—

Start writing...

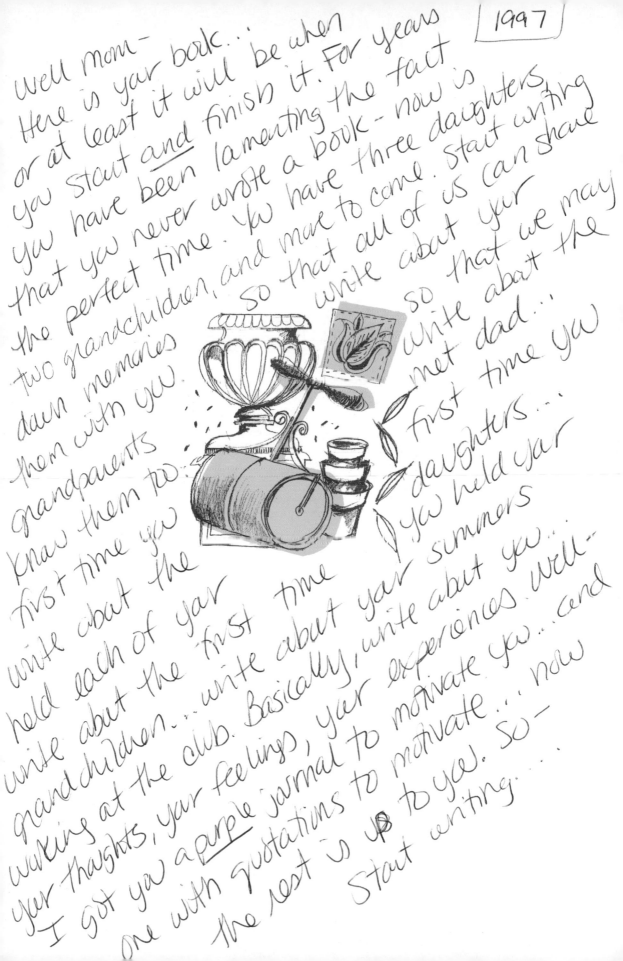

© 1997 by Running Press

Illustrations © 1997 by Jacqueline Mair
All rights reserved under the Pan-American and International Copyright Conventions

Printed in Hong Kong

*This book may not be reproduced in whole or in part, in any form or by any means, electronic
or mechanical, including photocopying, recording, or by any information storage and retrieval system
now known or hereafter invented, without written permission from the publisher.*

9   8   7   6   5   4   3   2   1
Digit on the right indicates the number of this printing

ISBN 0-7624-0052-8

Designed by Corinda Cook
Edited by Elaine M. Bucher

This book may be ordered by mail from the publisher.
Please add $2.50 for postage and handling.
But try your bookstore first!

Running Press Book Publishers
125 South Twenty-second Street
Philadelphia, Pennsylvania 19103-4399

Meditations
A Woman's
Personal Journal,
with Quotations

RUNNING PRESS
PHILADELPHIA · LONDON

All you need is deep within you waiting to unfold and reveal itself.

All you have to do is be still and take time to seek for what is within . . .

Eileen Caddy
20th-century American spiritualist

*T*here are so many noises and pulls and competing demands in our lives that many of us never find out who we are. Learn to be quiet enough to hear the sound of the genuine within yourself so that you can hear it in other people.

Marian Wright Edelman
20th-century American children's advocate

. . . self-esteem starts out as a personal blessing,
but it becomes nothing less than an evolutionary force.

Gloria Steinem (b. 1934)
American writer and feminist

You can have anything you want if you want it desperately enough. You must want it with an exuberance that erupts through the skin and joins the energy that created the world.

Sheila Graham
20th–century American writer

Love yourself first and everything else falls into line . . .

Lucille Ball (1911–1989)
American entertainer

Real strength comes from knowing we can survive . . .

Carole Hyatt
20th–century American writer

Now, dazzled, I discovered that *my* capacities were real.
It was like finding a fortune in the lining of an old coat.

Joan Mills
20th-century American writer

. . . the moment when you first wake up in the morning is the most wonderful of the twenty-four hours. No matter how weary or dreary you may feel, you possess the certainty that . . . absolutely anything may happen.

Monica Baldwin (1896–1975)
English writer

I have a friend who lives by a three-word
philosophy: "Seize the moment." Just possibly,
she may be the wisest woman on this planet.

Erma Bombeck (1927–1996)
American writer and humorist

*A*rranging a bowl of flowers
in the morning can give a sense
of quiet in a crowded day—like
writing a poem, or saying a prayer.

Anne Morrow Lindbergh (b. 1906)
American writer

Peace is when life flowers.

Amrita Pritam (b. 1919)
Indian poet

Until you make peace with who you are,
you'll never be content with what you have.

Doris Mortman
20th–century American writer

Being you is all about *connection*, about being *real*.
When you are you, you *connect* with others.

Henriette Anne Klauser
20th-century American writer

*Caring for myself is not self-indulgence,
it is self-preservation . . .*

Audre Lorde
20th-century American writer

I hope for an environment where the investigation of self will not be looked upon as self-indulgent and self-centered, but rather as self-centering. If we are not centered in self, how can we be centered in our work and our expression of human life?

Shirley MacLaine (b. 1934)
American actress, entertainer, and writer

Serenity is a gift from you to you.

Dorothy Briggs
20th–century American writer

We meditate to discover our own identity, our right place in the scheme of the universe. Through meditation, we acquire and eventually acknowledge our connection to an inner power source that has the ability to transform our outer world.

Julia Cameron
20th-century American writer

I used to think that "personal growth" was like cake. It was nice, a dessert to the main course of life, but not necessary. Words like "human potential" and "self-fulfillment" smacked to me of Esalen retreats and pop psychology. Now, I see that growth is as vitally nourishing to our lives as bread.

Ellen Goodman (b. 1941)
American writer

Learn the craft of knowing how to open your heart and
to turn on your creativity. There's a light inside of you.

Judith Jamison (b. 1944)
American dancer

Mistakes are a fact of life. It's the response to the error that counts.

Nikki Giovanni (b. 1943)
American poet

Maybe one of these days I'll be able to give myself a gold star for being ordinary, and maybe one of these days I'll give myself a gold star for being extraordinary—for persisting. And maybe one day I won't need to have a star at all.

Sue Bender
20th-century American writer

The extraordinary days don't need gold stars.
But ordinary days sure can be brighter
with a shiny, five-pointed pat on the back.

Sarah Ban Breathnach
20th-century American writer

*Perfectionism is the voice of the oppressor, the enemy of the people.
It will keep you cramped and insane your whole life.*

Anne Lamott
20th-century American writer

*W*e rarely are conscious of those primitive anxieties that creep out from under reason. And the only way to banish them is to turn on all the lights.

Patricia D. Cornwell (b. 1956)
American writer

Normal is absolutely my least favorite word. It is a statistical and conventional approximation, no more. When my mother was young, it was not normal to have intellectual ambitions, if one was a girl. . . . Normal is what sells fashions and face creams and other consumer items.

Amanda Cross (b. 1926)
American writer

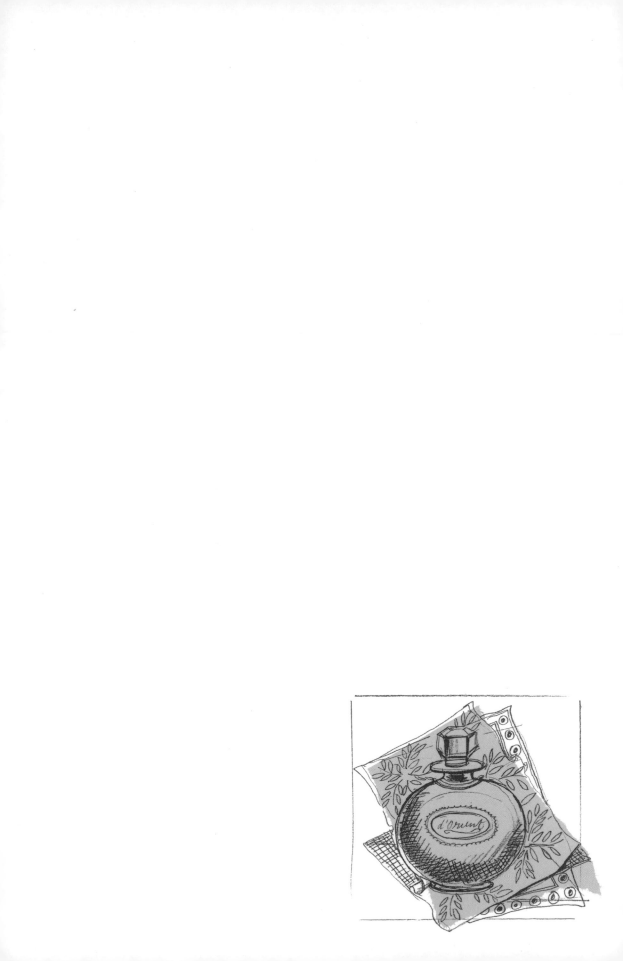

What a boon disparity is—difference of opinion has never been sufficiently appreciated. It is the unexpected, the unknowable, the divine irrationality of life that saves us.

Florida Scott-Maxwell (1883–1978)
American writer

*P*erhaps it would be easier if the stuff of our lives were cut from a uniform social and familial pattern, even if the cloth is not the pattern we would have designed for ourselves. Easier maybe, but not so beautiful or well suited to our particular needs, desires, and circumstances.

Hillary Rodham Clinton (b. 1947)
American First Lady

*When a form that you choose doesn't fit,
have the courage to change it.*

Claudia Bepko and Jo-Ann Krestan
20th-century American writers and therapists

*C*hallenges make you discover things about yourself that you never really knew. They're what make the instrument stretch—what make you go beyond the norm.

Cicely Tyson (b. 1939)
American actress

I think it's the end of progress if you stand still and think of what you've done in the past. I keep on.

Leslie Caron (b. 1931)
French actress

I've dreamt in my life dreams that have stayed with me ever after, and changed my ideas; they've gone through and through me, like wine through water, and altered the color of my mind.

Emily Brontë (1818–1848)
English writer

I have discovered the meaning of life. It resides in the books I love and the animals that surround me; in present friends and in memories of lovers and enemies, too; in silk, champagne, an applewood fire, and Mozart. It resides in what I can wrest from each day that I live.

Nancy Thayer (b. 1943)
American writer

I hope we realize there is never a reason
to sit alone in a dark room. . . . May we
never be too practical to burn a candle.

Erma Bombeck (1927–1996)
American writer and humorist

*I don't believe makeup and the right hairstyle alone
can make a woman beautiful. The most radiant woman
in the room is the one full of life and experience.*

Sharon Stone (b. 1958)
American actress

There is no cosmetic for beauty like happiness.

Marguerite Gardiner, Countess of Blessington (1789–1849)
Irish writer

Taking joy in life is a woman's best cosmetic.

Rosalind Russell (1912–1976)
American actress

The world is terrified of joyful women.
Make a stand. Be one anyway.

Marianne Williamson (b. 1952)
American writer and lecturer

. . . it isn't far off the mark to say
joy begets joy: We enjoy the rush, and
we're motivated to recapture the sensation.

Eileen Stukane
20th–century American writer

. . . life is like fording a river, stepping from one slippery
stone to another, and you must rejoice every time you don't lose
your balance, and learn to laugh at all the times you do.

Merle Shain
20th-century Canadian writer

. . . I'm learning to be happy with what I've got and who I am. . . . I've realized that I've got everything I need inside me; we all do.

Terry McMillan (b. 1951)
American writer

Be honest, when was the last time you leaped out of bed, threw open the window, and said, "Thank god I'm alive! This is the most glorious day, and today I'm going to do something so fabulous it will change my *entire life*"?

Katherine Neville (b. 1945)
American writer

Why not seize the pleasure at once?
How often is happiness destroyed
by preparation, foolish preparation!

Jane Austen (1775–1817)
English writer

I meditate, I do yoga, and I have a lot of friends
who are healers. . . . And if none of that works,
I go buy a chocolate bar and a bottle of cognac.

Susan Strasberg (b. 1938)
American actress

Deep within you is everything that is perfect,
ready to radiate through you and out into the world.

Diane Cirincione
20th–century American lecturer

There aren't any right or wrong emotions.
We feel what we feel.

P. D. James (b. 1920)
English writer

We can only learn to love by loving.

Iris Murdoch (b. 1919)
Irish writer

Joy is prayer—Joy is strength—Joy is love. . . . A joyful heart is the inevitable result of a heart burning with love.

Mother Teresa of Calcutta (b. 1910)
Founder, Missionaries of Charity

The human spirit is virtually indestructible, and its ability to rise from the ashes remains as long as the body draws breath.

Alice Miller
20th-century American writer

No set goal achieved satisfies. Success only breeds a new goal.
The golden apple devoured has seeds. It is endless.

Bette Davis (1908–1989)
American actress

To seek visions, to dream dreams, is essential, and it is also essential to try new ways of living, to make room for serious experimentation, to respect the effort even where it fails.

Adrienne Rich (b. 1929)
American poet, writer, and educator

Oh, it's delightful to have ambitions. . . . And there never seems to be any end to them—that's the best of it. Just as soon as you attain one ambition you see another one glittering higher up still. It does make life so interesting.

L. M. Montgomery (1874–1942)
Canadian writer

Everyone must dream. We dream to give ourselves hope. To stop dreaming—well, that's like saying you can never change your fate.

Amy Tan (b. 1952)
American writer

Today carve out a quiet interlude for
yourself in which to dream, pen in hand.

Sarah Ban Breathnach
20th-century American writer

Writing becomes an act of compassion toward life, the life we so often refuse to see because if we look too closely or feel too deeply, there may be no end to our suffering. But words empower us, move us beyond our suffering, and set us free.

Terry Tempest Williams
20th-century American naturalist

Certain springs are tapped only when we are alone. . . . Women need solitude in order to find again the true essence of themselves; that firm strand which will be the indispensable center of a whole web of human relationships.

Anne Morrow Lindbergh (b. 1906)
American writer

I have time to think. That is the great, greatest luxury.
I have time to be. Therefore my responsibility is huge.
To use time well and to be all that I can. . . .

May Sarton (1912–1995)
Belgian–born American writer and poet

Even in the grimmest of circumstances,
a shift in perspective can create startling change.

Susan Griffin (b. 1943)
American writer and poet

Sometimes it's better to talk about difficult subjects lying down; the change in posture sort of tilts the world so you can get a different angle on things.

Mary Willis Walker
20th-century American writer

Each person deserves a day away in which no problems are confronted, no solutions searched for. Each of us needs to withdraw from the cares which will not withdraw from us. We need hours of aimless wandering or spates of time sitting on park benches, observing the mysterious world of ants and the canopy of treetops.

Maya Angelou (b. 1928)
American writer, poet, and actress

. . . the imagination needs moodling—long, inefficient, happy idling, dawdling and puttering.

Barbara Ueland (1891–1985)
American writer

Bed is *not* a shameful, shiftless place
to be by day, nor is it necessary
to run a fever of 102 to deserve it.

Barbara Holland (b. 1925)
American writer

Silence and solitude are confrontational.
They plunge us instantly into truth,
and it is for this reason they are
so essential to the health of our spirit.

Barbara De Angelis (b. 1951)
American writer, therapist, and lecturer

Life can hurt us, but it does not hurt nearly so much if we have learned to listen to ourselves and to recognize how fully and richly we are trying to tell ourselves the truth.

Eugene Kennedy
20th–century American writer

*T*here is always something truly . . . restorative, really, finally comforting, in learning what is true. In coming to the end of an illusion, a false hope.

Sue Miller (b. 1943)
American writer

*Knowledge for its own sake—it's a very pure concept. I think
we all get too caught up in doing instead of just being sometimes. . . .*

Anne Rivers Siddon (b. 1936)
American writer

I feel that one must deliberate and then act, must scan every life choice with rational thinking but then base the decision on whether one's heart will be in it. No other person can tell you if your heart is involved, and logic cannot provide an answer.

Jean Shinoda Bolen (b. 1938)
American writer and psychiatrist

Knowledge is not power. Getting the right information and learning to apply it to your life is power.

Susan Powter (b. 1957)
American writer

You don't get to choose how you're going to die. Or when. You can only decide how you're going to live. Now.

Joan Baez (b. 1941)
American folk singer and composer

Find out who you are,
then do it on purpose.

Dolly Parton (b. 1946)
American singer

Life seems to love the liver of it.

Maya Angelou (b. 1928)
American writer, poet, and actress

Life is a great big canvas, and you should splash
all the paint on it that you can!

Carol Rae
20th-century American artist

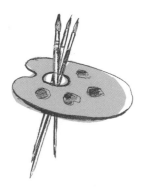